SCIENCE VIEW

SOUND

©2005 by Chelsea House Publishers, a subsidiary of Haights Cross Communications.

A Haights Cross Communications Company

Printed and bound in China.
10 9 8 7 6 5 4 3 2 1

Library of Congress Cataloging-in-Publication Data applied for.

ISBN: 0-7910-8210-5

Chelsea House Publishers

2080 Cabot Blvd. West, Suite 201
Langhorne, PA 19047-1813

http://www.chelseahouse.com

Produced by

David West 🧍🧍 **Children's Books**
7 Princeton Court
55 Felsham Road
London SW15 1AZ

Designer: Rob Shone
Editor: Gail Bushnell
Picture Research: Carlotta Cooper

PHOTO CREDITS :
Abbreviations: t-top, m-middle, b-bottom, r-right, l-left, c-center.

Front cover - tr, bl - Corbis Images. Pages 3 & 6t, 4–5, 8t, 11b, 16, 16–17, 18 both, 20, 21bl & br, 26–27, 27b, 28 both, 29t - Corbis Images. 6b (Nature Shell 0496), 9t (Pocket Watch 0876), 10t (Speaker System 007): budgetstockphoto.com. 7r, 13 both - NASA. 12t, 15 both - National Oceanic & Atmospheric Administration (NOAA). 12–13 Castrol. 14, 17t, 19, 29bl - Rex Features Ltd. 20br - Dover Books. 24t - Stock Images. 24–25 - Katz Pictures.

With special thanks to the models: Felix Blom, Tucker Bryant and Margaux Monfared.

An explanation of difficult words can be found in the glossary on page 31.

SCIENCE VIEW
SOUND

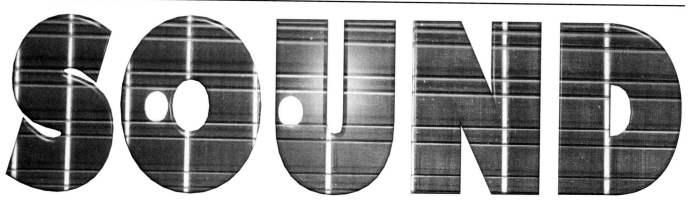

Steve Parker

CHELSEA HOUSE
PUBLISHERS
A Haights Cross Communications Company

CONTENTS

INTRODUCTION

Sssh! What's that sound? All around us are noises and sounds of every kind. Some are pleasing, like our favorite music and friendly voices. Some are worrying, like an emergency siren or a cry of pain. Sounds affect daily life in countless ways. Sound science, known as acoustics, is a vast area— and a huge business, too!

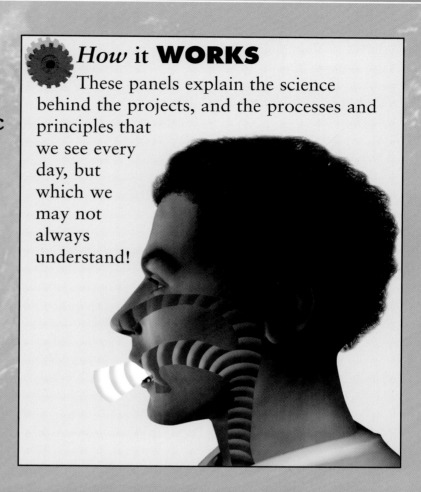

How it **WORKS**

These panels explain the science behind the projects, and the processes and principles that we see every day, but which we may not always understand!

PROJECT PANEL

The projects are simple to do with supervision, using household items. Remember—scientists are cautious. They prepare equipment thoroughly, they know what should happen, and they *always* put safety first.

Sound waves spread out from their source like ripples on a pond, but sounds move in all directions—upward and downward, too.

Sound is not a substance itself, but the way that a substance moves. Usually, the substance is air, through which sounds travel to our ears.

HIGHS AND LOWS

A sound travels through air as regions of high and low air pressure, following each other very quickly. High pressure is where the tiniest particles that make up air, called atoms, are pushed closer together. Low pressure is where they are pulled farther apart.

SOUND SOURCE

An object that makes a sound, such as a bell, is a sound source. Tap a bell and it shakes to and fro very rapidly, or vibrates. The vibrations push and pull the air around the bell and make it vibrate, too, as regions of high and low air pressure. These travel outward and are known as sound waves.

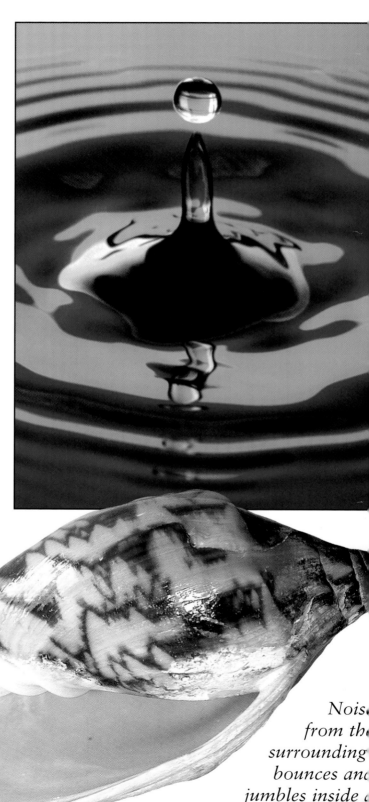

Nois. from th. surrounding bounces and jumbles inside shell, sounding like the sea

SOUND AS ENERGY

Sounds can travel as vibrations not only through air, but through many other substances and materials. These include liquids like water and hard solids such as glass and metal. The movements of atoms and other tiny particles in these substances represent energy. So sound is a form of energy, too.

Quiet sounds have less energy and travel shorter distances, so we have to place our ears nearer to hear them.

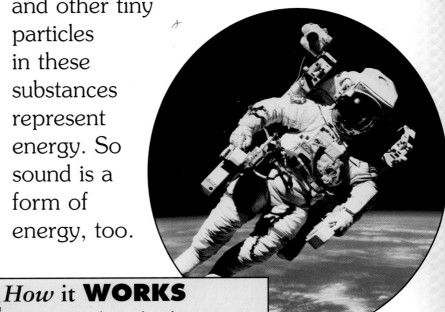

Sounds only travel if a substance carries them. Space is totally empty (a vacuum), even of air, and so it is silent.

PAPER CUP TELEPHONE

Stand a few yards from a friend and talk quietly. Can you be heard? Talk into a plastic cup joined by taut string to another cup, which your friend holds to his or her ear. Can you be heard now?

Paper cup

String

How it WORKS

Voice sounds make the cup vibrate, and the movements pass along the tight string to vibrate the other cup, too. Sound waves resemble a "Slinky®" spring, with the highs and lows of air pressure like the coils nearer and farther apart.

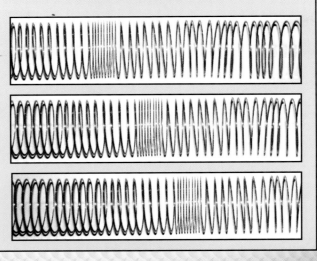

Knot string inside cup

7

On a summer day, grass rustles and bees hum, then there's a CRASH of thunder. Sounds vary greatly in their loudness, or volume.

MEASURING LOUDNESS

The loudness of a sound is indicated by measurements called decibels, dB. These units actually measure a sound's energy intensity, but this is usually similar to its overall volume.

BOOM! Explosions like a warship's guns firing are some of the biggest noises, at more than 130 dB on the loudness scale.

A passenger jet taking off can be as loud as 120 dB.

ODD SCALE

The quietest sounds that we can hear are 10 dB. Talking is 40–60 dB, and a loud truck or train is over 80 dB. However, the decibel scale can be misleading. Each increase of 10 dB, such as from 30 to 40 dB, means a huge ten-fold increase. Sounds over 90 dB can harm hearing, especially if they are high-pitched and long-lasting.

SOUND CANNON

Sudden, loud sounds have enough energy to make "wind" that can move objects by changing air pressure.

Make a cardboard tube and tape thin plastic over one end. Flick this hard to make a cracking noise. See light objects, like hanging popcorn, "dance!"

A quietly ticking watch measures only 20 dB. A jackhammer at 100 dB is not five times louder, but 100 million times the volume.

How it **WORKS**

Sound waves travel outward through air in all directions from a source. They gradually spread and lose their energy—unless stopped by objects around. In the sound cannon, the tube funnels all the sound waves in the same direction, out of the end. This keeps their energy concentrated into a narrow "beam."

String

Popcorn on strings | Sound waves | Cardboard tube | Flick end sharply

Sounds have "height." A bird's tweet is high or shrill, while a lion's roar is low or deep. This feature of sound is known as pitch or frequency.

WAVES PER SECOND

A sound's pitch depends on how many times the sound source vibrates per second, sending out one sound wave each time. It is measured in units called Hertz, Hz. One Hz is one vibration per second.

As a kettle boils, the steam moves faster and makes the whistle vibrate more rapidly, so its pitch rises.

A speaker cabinet has different-sized loudspeakers for various pitches. The large woofer emits the low notes. The tiny tweeter sends out the highest ones.

SLIDE WHISTLE

Smaller objects generally vibrate faster than larger ones, making higher-pitched sounds. Altering the length of a tube changes the pitch of its sound. Trombones and some other musical instruments work in this way.

You can make a slide whistle from two different-size tubes of cardboard.

Blow gentl straight acros the open end

Slide th thicke outer tub up an down th thinne inner tube

he lower or deeper a sound,
e longer its waves. A ship's
ooming foghorn has sound
aves tens of yards long.

How it **WORKS**

Blowing across the
whistle's end
makes the whole
tube vibrate, along
with the air inside
it. The longer this
air column, the
longer the sound
waves it produces,
and the lower
their frequency,
and so the deeper
the pitch. For best
results, hold the
whistle gently so
the tube can
vibrate freely.

High pitch or
frequency sound
(shorter wave)

Low pitch or
frequency sound
(longer wave)

THE SOUND SPECTRUM

Our ears hear a limited range, or spectrum,
of pitches. The deepest sounds we detect, like
thunder, are about 25 Hz. The shrillest, like
the "hiss" of a cymbal, are up to 20,000 Hz.
The note halfway up the musical scale,
known as middle C, is 256 Hz.

A hippo's roar deepens as the animal grows, because its
throat and mouth enlarge and so vibrate more slowly.

Thunder and lightning are made by the same giant spark of electricity. Why do we see the flash before hearing the clap?

SPEEDS COMPARED

The reason is that sound travels more slowly than light—a million times slower. Sound's speed in air is about 1,115 feet (340 m) per second, 760 mph (1,226 km/h). So thunder's boom takes five seconds for one mile of distance, while lightning's flash takes almost no time.

MORE SPEEDS OF SOUND

Sound's speed varies with temperature and pressure. At great heights, where the air is cold and thin, it is 968 feet (295 m) per second. Also, sound travels much faster in liquids and solids than it does in air. Its speed is 4,921 feet (1,500 m) per second in water; 16,404 (3.1 miles) in steel; and 18,044 (3.4 miles) in glass.

Count the seconds from the flash of the lightning to the bang of the thunder, and divide by five, to find out the storm's distance from you in miles.

BURSTING BALLOONS

You can show how light goes faster than sound by bursting a balloon. Look and listen as a friend, standing about 115 feet (35 m) away, holds an inflated balloon and pricks with pin—POP! What do you see and hear?

The first land vehicle to go supersonic was the Thrust SSC jet-car in 1997, reaching 761.3 mph (1,227.9 km/h).

The first supersonic craft was the Bell X-1 rocket plane. It broke the "sound barrier" in 1947, piloted by Charles "Chuck" Yeager.

SUPERSONIC

Speeds faster than sound are supersonic. In air, this causes shock waves of air pressure to build up and create the massive deep thud of a "sonic boom."

How it **WORKS**

Sound from balloon

Observer

Light from balloon

Light waves from the balloon travel the 115 feet (35 m) almost instantly. Sound waves take about one-tenth of a second. So you see the balloon burst before you hear the POP.

As a supersonic plane flies, air cannot get out of the way fast enough. Pressure waves build up and crash into one another, and are heard all around as a deep boom.

13

To the motorcycle racer, the engine's whine is constant. To others, it falls in pitch when going past: "Neeaaow!"

The change in pitch is easie: to hear with high sounds, like emergency vehicle sirens, rather than low ones

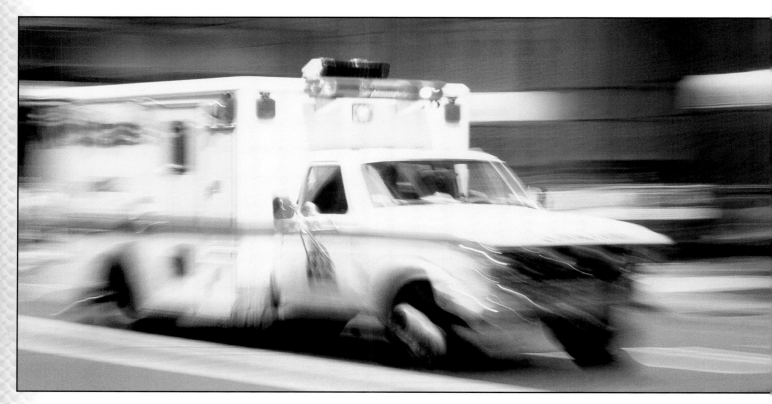

A Strange Effect

This effect is heard if a sound source moves in relation to a listener. The source emits a steady frequency of waves. But because it moves slightly between sending out each one, the waves bunch up ahead and are farther apart behind.

WHOO-WHOO SIREN

Tin can attached to string
Twirl can at constant rate.

Tie a can to a six-foot (2 m) piec of string. In an open and safe place swing the can around at a stead speed. Air passing the open en: makes the can vibrate and produc a noise. You should hear the sam pitch if the can twirls at a constan speed—but what does it sound lik to a friend standing nearby

HIGH TO LOW

As these sound waves reach a listener nearby, they are high in pitch as the source approaches. Then, as it passes, the pitch falls. This is the Doppler effect. It works not only with sound waves but with other kinds of waves, too, such as radar waves and light waves.

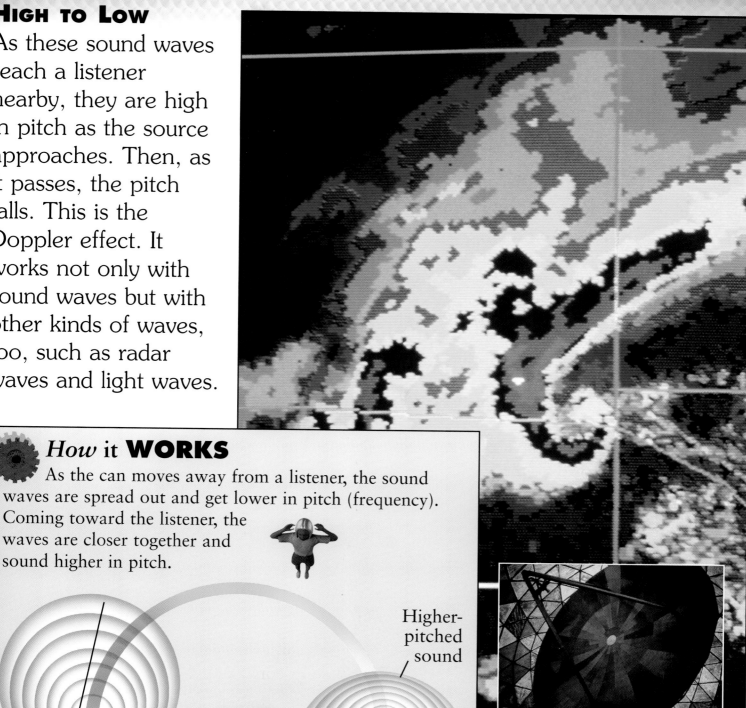

How it WORKS

As the can moves away from a listener, the sound waves are spread out and get lower in pitch (frequency). Coming toward the listener, the waves are closer together and sound higher in pitch.

Higher-pitched sound

Lower-pitched sound

Radar dishes at some weather stations use radar waves, and the way they alter with the Doppler effect, to detect the movement and density of clouds (inset). They can then make weather maps (above).

15

If sound waves hit a surface, what happens depends on the nature of the surface. If it's hard and smooth, the waves bounce off or reflect. We call this an echo . . . echo . . . echo . . .

A GAP OF TIME

Like light reflecting off a mirror, sounds reflect best off hard, flat, smooth surfaces such as walls and floors. We only hear the echo separately if it comes back to our ears more than one-tenth of a second after the original sound finishes. Due to the speed of sound, this means the surface must be at least 56–66 feet (17–20 m) away for a clear echo.

Dolphins make clicks and squeaks and detect waterborne echoes from objects around to find their prey.

TICK-TOCK ECHO-CLOCK

Put a clock with a loud tick-tock at one end of a long cardboard tube, placed at an angle near a hard surface like a wall. Place another tube so their two ends are close, as shown. Adjust the second tube's angle. Suddenly, the sound from its end is louder.

Bats produce very high-pitched, or ultrasonic, sound waves and hear the reflections from objects as small as gnats and midges.

liffs and big rocks
e natural sound
flectors, so canyons
re full of echoes.

ADING AWAY

s a sound travels, its waves
pread out, or dissipate. Their energy
asses into the surroundings, changed
to heat and other forms of energy.
o, the sound's volume decreases with
istance. When sound waves hit a
urface, they lose energy, too, so an
cho is quieter than its original sound.

Like sound waves, radio waves reflect off objects. This is how radar works, so air traffic control can track planes.

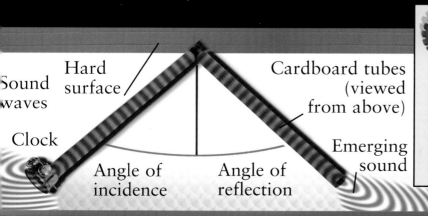

Sound waves

Hard surface

Clock

Angle of incidence

Cardboard tubes (viewed from above)

Emerging sound

Angle of reflection

How it **WORKS**

Sounds bounce off hard surfaces at the same angle they hit it. In scientific terms, the angle of incidence equals the angle of reflection. When this happens, the sound reflects best into the second tube and is loudest.

A frog vibrates part of its throat to make a croaking sound.

If there were no people, the world would still be noisy. There are countless natural sounds, especially from the weather and from a vast variety of animals.

Birds have a larynx-like part in the lower windpipe called the syrinx.

TO AND FRO

Most animals make sounds by vibrating thin, flexible body parts to and fro. We do this, too. Our sound-makers are called vocal cords. They are like two narrow flaps that stick out from the voice box, or larynx, in the neck. To speak, muscles move the cords almost together. Air coming up from the lungs passes through the narrow gap between them, making them vibrate.

ELASTIC BAND GUITAR

You can make a "guitar" from a box and some elastic bands! The box needs a sound hole. Stretch the bands between two sets of corks to form a "bridge" and "nut" like a real guitar. These hold the bands off the box so they can vibrate. Arrange the bands in the order of their length when they are not stretched.

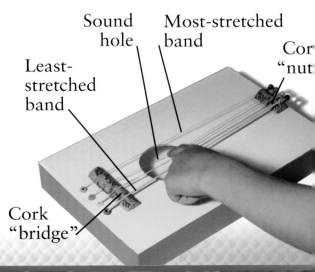

Sound hole

Most-stretched band

Least-stretched band

Cork "nut"

Cork "bridge"

Grasshoppers rub tiny, tooth-like pegs spaced along their rear legs against a hardened, rod-like vein in the wing, making the wing vibrate.

SHORTER, TIGHTER, HIGHER

A sound's pitch depends on how fast its source vibrates. In general, shorter items vibrate faster than longer ones. Most women have shorter vocal cords, 0.6–0.8 inch (15–20 mm), compared to most men, at 0.8–1 inch (20–25 mm). So women's voices are slightly higher-pitched. Also, stiff or tightly stretched items vibrate faster than loose, floppy ones.

How it **WORKS**

Just as vibrations from the vocal cords travel to the mouth, sound waves from the band's vibrations pass into the air, and through the sound hole into the box. Here, they bounce or reflect and make the box vibrate, too, giving off extra sound waves to make the sound louder. The tighter an elastic band is stretched, the higher its vibrating frequency when twanged.

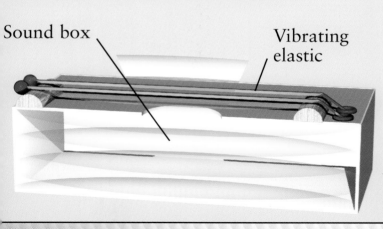

Sound box

Vibrating elastic

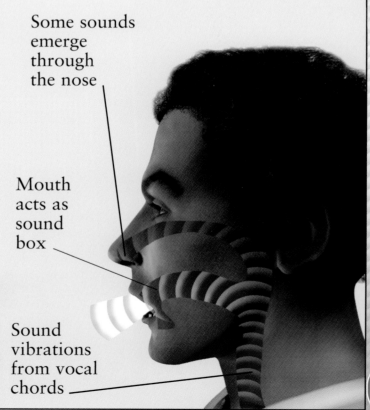

Some sounds emerge through the nose

Mouth acts as sound box

Sound vibrations from vocal chords

There's a very simple way of describing a sound. It's something we can hear!

HEAR, EAR!

Ears are energy converters. They change the energy of sound waves into tiny pulses of electrical energy called nerve signals. These are then sent to the brain, which identifies the sounds.

An owl's ears are set wide apart and at slightly different heights. This makes pinpointing a sound from prey at night very precise.

How it **WORKS**

Sound waves enter the ear and hit the eardrum. This passes vibrations along three tiny bones to the curly-shaped cochlea. Inside, the vibrations shake thousands of microscopic hairs to generate nerve signals.

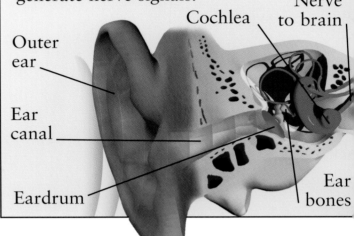

Outer ear

Ear canal

Eardrum

Cochlea

Nerve to brain

Ear bones

WHERE'S THE SOUND?

A sound from the side reaches one ear before the other. Sound's speed means the time difference is only about one-thousandth of a second, but the ears and brain detect this, so we know where the sound comes from. This is called stereophonic hearing.

How it **WORKS**

Low-pitched sounds like ship foghorns tend to echo more and spread out wider than high-pitched ones. It can be difficult to judge their direction. Sailors used to lengthen "ear-to-ear" distance using sound funnels, to increase the time gap between a sound reaching them. By turning around, a ship's fog-horn could be pinpointed.

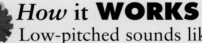

"ONE-TWO, ONE-TWO"

Devices that "hear" are microphones. They are similar to ears because they turn sound waves into tiny electrical signals. Some types use crystals. Others use a coil of wire vibrating near a magnet to make the signals.

FEELING SOUNDS

Animals like earthworms and scorpions have no ears for airborne sounds. Yet they can detect our approach. They feel the vibrations of our footsteps carried through the ground—the same vibrations that start the sound waves we hear through air.

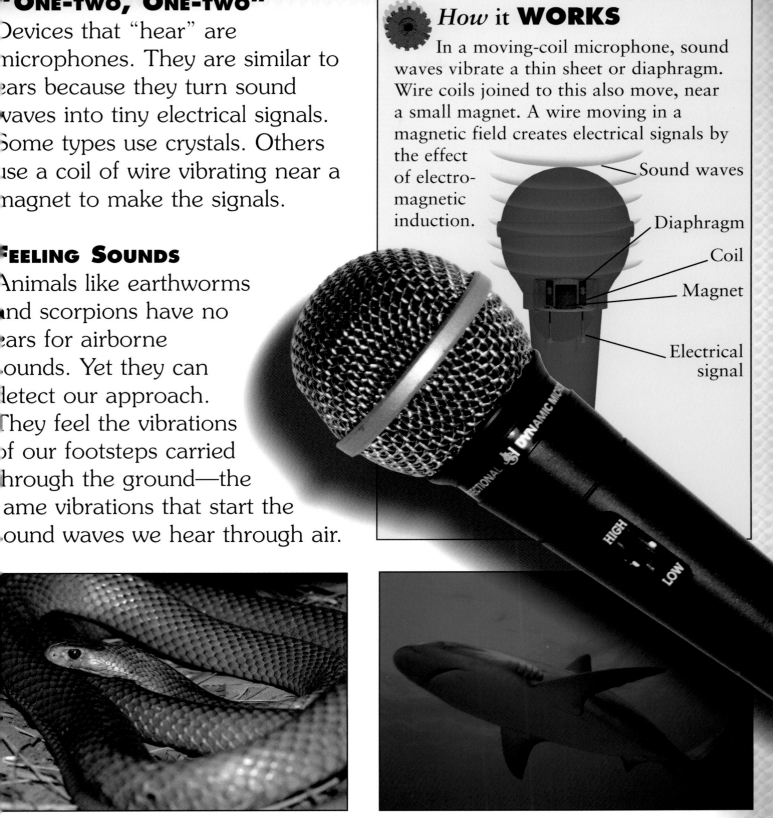

How it WORKS

In a moving-coil microphone, sound waves vibrate a thin sheet or diaphragm. Wire coils joined to this also move, near a small magnet. A wire moving in a magnetic field creates electrical signals by the effect of electro-magnetic induction.

Sound waves
Diaphragm
Coil
Magnet
Electrical signal

Most snakes have ears, but these work poorly. A snake relies more on feeling vibrations from the ground along its body.

Sounds travel in the sea as ripples of water pressure. Fish detect these and other currents using the lateral line sense along their sides.

Many of the sounds we hear each day are not "live." They were made some time ago. They have been stored, or recorded, to play back later—as many times as we wish.

Firs
to recor
sounds wa
invento
Thomas Edison
in 1877. Hi
"phonograph
made wav
grooves in th
hard-wa.
coating o
a cylinde

HERE'S ONE WE MADE EARLIER

The first method of recording sound "captured" the pattern of waves in physical form. The waves hit a thin sheet or diaphragm attached to a hard metal point, the stylus. This gouges a wavy pattern in a hard-wax or plastic-like surface. Playback works in the reverse way. Vinyl discs use this technology.

A typical LP (long-playing) vinyl disk has a V-shaped groove about 1,640 feet (500 m) long on each side.

How it WORKS

A vinyl disk has one long groove per side, spiraling from edge to center. As the disk rotates, waves in the groove vibrate the needle-shaped stylus pressing into it. In an original gramophone, the vibrations pass up to a flexible sheet, the diaphragm, which produces the sound waves.

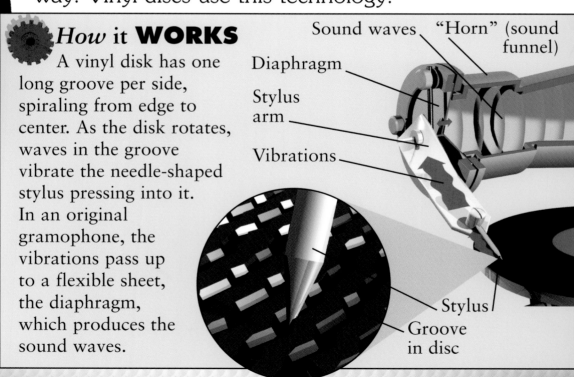

Sound waves
"Horn" (sound funnel)
Diaphragm
Stylus arm
Vibrations
Stylus
Groove in disc

After sounds and music have been turned into electrical signals, they can be altered and merged together at the studio mixing desk.

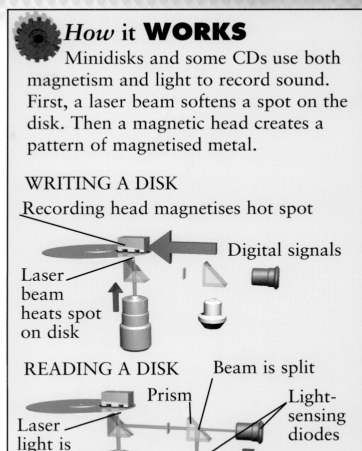
MODERN SOUND

A century later, a new method was devised using light—the compact disc, or CD. It has about 3,000 million microscopic bowl-shaped pits in its surface. As it spins, the pits and flat areas between move past a laser beam. Pits do not reflect the beam but "flats" do. Over half a million reflections per second are detected by sensors and used as digital code to make the sounds. DVDs work in the same way.

MP3 and similar formats store sounds as electronic files on microchips. Files can be moved from a computer to a personal player.

Some sounds are pleasing to most people. The different pitches or frequencies relate in a tuneful and melodic way. These are the sounds of music.

SCALES

The different pitches of a musical scale are called notes. They rise in a regular way: "do, re, mi, fa, so, la, ti, do." The frequencies of the notes relate to each other, such as one being twice another. When the notes are heard at the same time, they "fit" together. This is called harmony.

Music can be "stored" in written form, as note symbols on lines called staves.

Instruments played on their own, without needing extra energy, usually electricity, are called acoustic.

TONE AND TIMBRE

In a band or orchestra, if each instrument played the same note or frequency, it would be possible to distinguish a guitar from a trumpet or piano. This is due to tone or "timbre." An instrument produces not only the main frequency for the note, but also many related frequencies known as harmonics. Each instrument has its own combination of different harmonics at different volumes, which gives its unique sound.

An orchestra can contain more than a hundred instruments. Each may play different notes from a written version of the music, called the score. The composer and conductor ensure that, overall, the sounds blend together.

BOTTLE XYLOPHONE

With identical bottles in a row, you can make your own music. Add increasing amounts of water along the row. (Food coloring in the water helps you see its level.) Use a spoon to tap the bottles. Try glass and plastic bottles and metal cans for different sounds.

How it **WORKS**

A tap on the bottle makes it and the air inside it vibrate. The smaller the air volume, the faster it vibrates, so the sound waves given off are higher in pitch. Adjust the water levels for a musical scale.

Longer waves give lower pitch   Shorter waves give higher pitch

25

Noises are usually sounds that are not pleasing to the ear. They can be unwanted, harsh, irritating, grating, rumbling, squeaky—or just too loud!

FEATURES OF NOISE

Pleasant sounds tend to be made of frequencies that fit together, or harmonize, and change volume smoothly with a regular rhythm. Noisy sounds usually contain frequencies that are unrelated and jumbled, and change volume and start or stop at random.

NOISE ANNOYS

Noise can have great effects on daily life. If it continues for too long, even at low volume, it can be distracting and cause bad moods, headaches, and other problems. If it is loud, it can harm hearing.

How it WORKS

Soundproofing materials tend to be soft, flexible, and rough-surfaced. They absorb some sound wave energy and convert it to other forms, such as heat and movements within their own structure. They also reflect some of the waves so they can be absorbed later.

This acoustic research room has soft projections on all surfaces to jumble and absorb sounds, preventing reflections

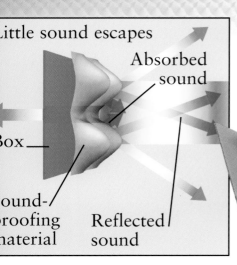

Little sound escapes

Absorbed sound

Box

Sound-proofing material

Reflected sound

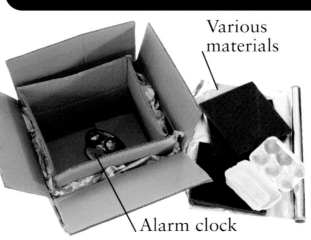

Various materials

Alarm clock

Test which common materials are soundproofers. Put an alarm clock with the alarm set in a box lined with one of the materials. Close the lid and assess the volume of the alarm. Which material is the best soundproofer?

Silencer boxes fitted to vehicles absorb sound energy from the engine's exhaust gases.

ANTI-SOUND

Materials and devices that lessen noise and other sounds are called soundproofing or sound insulation. They are used in houses, factories, and other buildings, as well as in cars, trains, and planes. Many, like foamed plastics, also insulate against heat.

Regulations state that soundproof headsets must be worn for certain jobs, to protect hearing.

27

All around us are sounds we cannot hear—they are pitched too high or low for our ears.

We can hear some of the underwater sounds made by whales, such as squeals and moans, but many other whale sounds especially fast clicks, are ultrasonic.

Too Low, Too High

As shown earlier, our ears detect sound waves with frequencies from about 25 to 20,000 Hz. There are sound waves outside this range, but we cannot hear them. The deepest, with frequencies below about 25 Hz, are called infrasounds. The highest, with frequencies above 20,000 Hz, are known as ultrasounds.

Elephants make extremely low infrasonic rumbles that are detected by herd members several miles away.

SES FOR
NHEARD SOUNDS

ery low and high
ounds have many
ses. The slow
ibrations of infrasound
an shake and test the
trength of structures
s large as bridges.
Jltrasounds are sent
ut as a narrow beam,
nd any reflections or
choes show the size
nd location of objects
n the surroundings—
rom enemy
ubmarines to babies.

Evidence is mounting that the powerful sound waves of submarine sonar cause various types of harm to whales.

How it **WORKS**

A medical ultrasound machine beams harmless high-pitched sound waves into the body. These reflect off parts inside in different ways. The reflections are analyzed by computers to form an image.

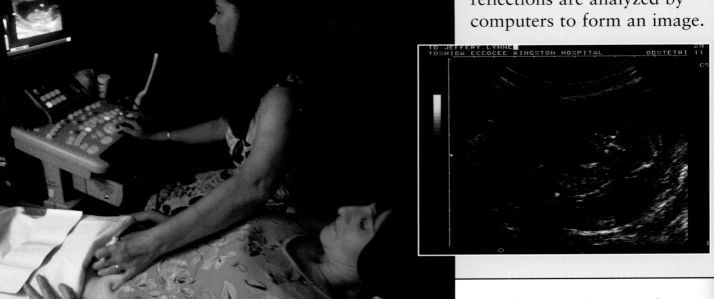

An ultrasound image shows a fetus in its mother's womb.

29

THE NATURE OF SOUND

Vibrations travelling through the air, or some other medium, are detected by the ear as sounds. Any type of motion is kinetic energy, so sound is kinetic energy, too. Sound is often pictured as traveling as up-and-down, or transverse, waves, as in the diagram below. In fact, it really travels as regions of high air pressure, where atoms and molecules of air are nearer together (compressed), alternating with regions of low air pressure, where the atoms and molecules are farther apart (rarefied). These are known as longitudinal waves and resemble the "Slinky®" spring shown on page 7.

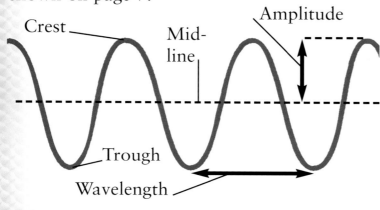

WAVELENGTH

The length of each wave varies according to the pitch of the sound. In a sound of constant pitch or note, all the waves have the same length. Here are some examples:
• Very low pitch from a big drum or bass guitar—each wave over 33 feet (10 m) long
• Note of middle C near the center of a piano keyboard—about 51 inches (130 cm)
• Baby's squeal—4–8 inches(10–20 cm)
• Just-audible bat squeak—0.6 inches (1.5 cm)

FREQUENCY

Frequency is a measure of how many waves go past per second and is measured in Hz (Hertz). As a sound's wavelength decreases,

more waves pass each second, so frequency increases. Some examples of frequencies:
• Human voice   average 75–1,600 H
• Growling lion   50–200 H
• Cat meow   700–1,500 H
• Bird song   2,000–12,000 H

AMPLITUDE AND VOLUME

The "height" of a sound wave is known as it amplitude and roughly corresponds to how far atoms and molecules move or vibrate as part of the wave. Even in the loudest sounds, this movement is just a fraction of an inch.

MACH SCALE

The speed of sound varies according to the substance it passes through and conditions like temperature. On the Mach scale, the speed of sound is 1. In air at sea level and a temperature of 68°F (20°C), Mach 1 is about 1,115 feet per second (340 m per s) or 760 mph (1,226 km/h). So a plane flying twice th speed is traveling at Mach 2, and so on.

THE DECIBEL SCALE

Sound's energy content, or intensity, is measured in decibels (dB), and is similar to volume or loudness (see also page 9).

10 dB	*Quietest sounds we can detect*
20 dB	*Whisper*
30 dB	*Quiet background sound*
40 dB	*Quiet talking*
50 dB	*Television at normal volume*
60 dB	*Loud conversation*
70 dB	*Vacuum cleaner, electric drill*
80 dB	*Train rushing past platform*
90 dB	*Heavy traffic on highway*
100 dB	*Jackhammer, sawmill saw*

GLOSSARY

acoustic
Having to do with sound. Also, when a musical instrument's sound is not amplified electronically.

Doppler effect
When a sound source moves in relation to the listener, so the sound seems higher pitched as the source comes nearer and lower pitched as it travels away.

frequency
Speed at which a process or item repeats itself, such as the number of sound waves passing a place in one second, measured in Hz.

infrasonic
Sound waves with pitches or frequencies below the range of human hearing, usually lower than 10–25 Hz (waves per second).

larynx
The voice box in the neck, containing the vocal cords, where the sounds of the voice, known as vocalizations, are made.

reflect
To bounce off or back, as when sound waves bounce off a wall as an echo, or light rays reflect off a mirror to form an image.

sonar
The sound version of radar, in which sound waves are sent out, and reflections (echoes) from objects are analyzed to show the object's size and position.

supersonic
Faster than the speed of sound. This varies according to the substance sound is passing through and conditions such as temperature (see opposite page).

ultrasonic
Sound waves with pitches or frequencies above the range of human hearing, usually higher than 20,000 Hz (waves per second).

vibration
When an object moves to and fro from a central or middle position.

31